THE
LITTLE BOOK
OF
GIANT PUNS
BRING BIG LAUGHS
EVERYWHERE

By
Benjamin Branfman

1. One time, a detective solved a crime by shattering his cellphone cover. I guess you could say he really cracked the case.

2. I once trained a student to have fantastic eyesight. She was definitely my best pupil.

3. Did you hear about the tightrope walker who had credit card debt? I guess you could say she had some outstanding balance.

4. One time, a car salesman sold the final car on his lot. It was actually a great car, and the owner paid in full. In other words, the car was last but not leased.

5. Did you hear about the chemical flask that earned a diploma? I guess you could say it was a graduated cylinder.

6. I thought about writing a book about books, because it seemed like a novel idea.

7. One time, I used alphabet soup as the spine for a book. The end result was mesmerizing; or, should I say, spellbinding?

8. One time, I bought a male deer for a dollar. So in this situation, I guess you could say the buyer and the seller both got a buck.

9. Did you hear about the man who attacked the Energizer Bunny? Police are charging him with battery.

10. My roommate and I want to buy a hot tub for our apartment. I think that we can afford one if we "pool" our resources.

11. My friend recently invented a smartphone the size of a pill. So, I guess you could say the phone is more of a tablet.

12. One time, when I had stomach pain, I deduced that I needed to go to the bathroom, because I had ruled out every other possibility. In other words, I guess you could say that I embraced the process of elimination.

13. Did you hear about the lawyer who held a crucifix under a microscope? I guess you could say he performed a cross examination.

14. Did you hear about the tied piece of string that was convicted of a misdemeanor? I guess you could say the verdict was knot guilty.

15. I used to have two baby dogs who would only stop barking while they were eating deep-fried cornmeal cakes. So, I guess you could say that the cakes were hushpuppies.

16. Did you hear about the celebrity whose house was supported by a giant wind turbine? I guess you could say she had a strong fan base.

17. One time, an evil mastermind's plan fell apart when his patch of land was covered in aluminum. In other words, I guess you could say his plot was foiled.

18. Did I tell you about that time when I had a lot of difficulty bartering for metal? I guess you could say it was quite an "ore deal."

19. Did you hear about the rattlesnake that returned a stolen jewel from a robbery? It must have been a diamondback.

20. What do you call a blimp whose passenger is an attractive princess? A hot heir balloon.

21. Did you hear about the celebrity who became famous for sprinting in circles around a flour factory? I guess you could say that, despite his fame, he still had a run-of-the-mill job.

22. Did you hear about the Olympic athlete who built a bank safe out of metal pipe? I guess her event was the pole vault.

23. Did you hear about the supervillain who had the power to make people give confessions in public movie theaters? His name was General Admission.

24. Did you hear about the sauté dish that received negative reviews from critics? I guess you could say it was panned.

25. Once in a very long while, you can find a raw piece of steak that predicts the future accurately. So I guess you could say, when it comes to beef, you find a rare medium well done.

26. The most disgusting thing that I ever saw was at a grocery store. No matter how gross anything else is, this was definitely grocer.

27. Did you hear about the Florida cop who invented a new type of screw clamp? He must have been working on Miami Vice.

28. One time, I used a needle and thread to weave a tapestry of a farm. Much to my surprise, the tapestry farm actually began to sprout stems of grain. So, I guess it really is true that you reap what you sew.

29. Did you know 99% of all statistics don't have insightful averages? I guess you could say they don't really "mean" much.

30. Whenever you fly to Hawaii, you get a wreath of flowers called a lei. But if your plane takes too long to depart, your wreath might get revoked. In other words, it's possible that your flight will be de-lei-ed.

31. A bunch of my mom's sisters founded a new settlement. In other words, I guess you could say they formed an aunt colony.

32. Did you hear about the camera that can only use special zoom settings during January 1st? I guess you could say the camera has some New Year's resolutions.

33. People who have food poisoning often stay on the toilet for a very long time. Afterward, they look very flushed.

34. After a dentist spent her life fighting tooth decay, her colleagues made a statue and a "plaque" in her honor.

35. I recently invented a way to store electronic data during difficult road trips. In other words, I found a secret to hard drives.

36. Did you hear about the man who sold large amounts of pre-ripped jeans to retail stores? I guess you could say he was in the holesale business.

37. There once was a banking firm that gave all of its investors free soup, consisting of either chicken broth, vegetable broth, or fish broth. In other words, I guess you could say the banking firm gave several stock options.

38. Some people work very hard to put together instruction booklets. So, I guess you could say their work involves manual labor.

39. A farmer was getting bad cell phone reception in his fields, so he climbed up on a ladder and stood above his cattle. He got a better signal that way, but his neighbors could all eavesdrop on what he was saying. In other words, I guess you could say he was over-herd.

40. Bruce Lee, Jackie Chan, and Chuck Norris had a contest to see who could fight best, wielding a chain with a wooden bar on each end. Everyone expected Chuck Norris to destroy the competition, but Bruce and Jackie actually did better. Out of ten judges, five liked Bruce's fighting, five Jackie's, and nunchuks.

41. A rich man had a friend that he found so reliable, he made a special fund to support the friend financially. In other words, I guess you could say that the rich man found his friend to be trust-worthy.

42. It always takes me a long time to decide whether I like a certain mirror, because I need to reflect on it.

43. One of the most famous universities in Louisiana only has a single main road, with a narrow incoming side and a narrow outgoing side. In other words, I guess you could say it's a Tulane highway.

44. Doctors just invented a machine that lets people survive without hearts. I really hope these machines go into circulation.

45. One time, there was a crocodile who loved to tell stories. He also loved to attend barbecues before football games. So, I guess you could say this storytelling crocodile was really more of a tale-gator.

46. Did you know that King Henry IV of England once played a game of ten-pins without any money? I guess you could say he was Bolingbroke.

47. One time, I chose a day to get my window-shades installed, and then I went out to dinner with a woman I didn't know. In other words, I arranged blind dates.

48. I once knew an artist who ALWAYS based his work off things from the United Nations. Considering how he never changed his concepts, I'd say he was extremely UNinspired.

49. There once was a debater who always surrendered in arguments, but farmed lots of food. So, I guess you could say he reliably yielded.

50. Two pandas were caught in a time loop, where they had to live through the same events over and over again. You've probably heard this story before, but it bears repeating.

51. I once knew a man who was extremely nice to hotel staff, but quite rude to everyone else. In other words, I guess you could say he was very inn considerate.

52. Did you hear about the man who got out of prison during his trial, by giving a bundle of hay to a judge? I guess you could say he went out on bale.

53. Did you hear about the scam artist who made a guidebook to help other criminals plan out their schemes? In other words, he made a "con template."

54. Last night I ate some really tough bread, followed by some very grainy meat, followed by some extremely rough-skinned fruit. In other words, I guess you could say I ate a three coarse meal.

55. I once knew a chef who always signed letters by stamping a giant saucer down on the paper. After decades of doing this, the chef became more famous for his odd letter-signing habit than for his food. In other words, I guess you could say the saucer became his signature dish.

56. Nowadays, most startup music labels begin with a few friends making their songs in cheap one-room apartments. In other words, I guess you could say that not much has changed since the corporate days, because musicians still rely on a studio.

57. Did you know that, in real life, Bigfoot is actually a pumpkin gourd that likes sarcastic insults? That's how he earned the nickname 'Sass-squash.'

58. I once knew a man whose shoe was a mile long. For him, getting dressed was a big feat.

59. I have a friend who collects stamps and news articles. I guess you could say she likes to be kept posted.

60. I once knew a man who used a wheelchair as a hat. He had no physical disability, and the wheelchair fit very awkwardly on his head. In other words, he did not have a handy cap.

61. Poet E.E. Cummings wrote his name in all lower-case letters, as a way of making himself seem more unique. In other words, I guess you could say the lower-case letters helped him to capitalize on his work.

62. There once was a weaver who never felt that his work met the proper standards. In other words, I guess you could say that he found his threading un-seam-ly.

63. Did you hear about the man who searched all over the internet for pictures of people with big, bushy hair over their eyes? I guess you could say he wanted to eye-browse.

64. I once knew an evening security guard who liked to show up to work in a full suit of armor, and squirm around in his chair. Between the armor, the time of day, and the squirming, I'd say this guard was pulling a lot of knight shifts.

65. If popcorn could hold a position in the military, I'm guessing its rank would be kernel.

66. In the future, people will evolve so their brains can exist outside of their bodies. In the present day, there's actually one woman who can already do this; so basically, she's a head of her time.

67. Once at a baseball game, a pitcher decided to throw a giant eyeball instead of a baseball. The batter stayed calm, but still struck out. So, I guess you could say the hitter didn't bat an eye.

68. A friend of mine recently tore several holes in his short trousers. In other words, I guess you could say he was having a problem with his breeches.

69. If you knew a female monk who worked in the same profession as you, then what she did for a living would be "nun of your business."

70. Once, when I was eating Chinese food, I found a bent paper clip floating around in my noodles. Then, later, I found a rubber band buried in my vegetable fried rice. I never realized that office supplies were a "staple" of Chinese cuisine.

71. There once was a great leader who managed to treat and overcome his single weakness. In other words, I guess you could say he found his Achilles' heal.

72. I once knew a man who became very riled whenever he smelled a burning fragrance. In other words, I guess you could say that he got very incensed.

73. Did you hear about the tuxedo-maker who was sued for damages? I guess his tuxedos were more like suits.

74. Did you know that breath-fresheners stay crisp even if they're stored away for a long time? I guess you could say they stay in mint condition.

75. In the Old West, artists used to duel by seeing which person could sketch a revolver faster. So, I guess you could say the winner was the quicker person to draw a weapon.

76. I was reading a book about medieval times, when a knight magically jumped out of the story from his picture on the paper. I asked him what he had been before he became a knight; he replied that he had been a page.

77. No matter how politely I behave, whenever I look into a mirror, my reflection is always shooting saliva at people. My reflection must be my spitting image.

78. There once was a kingdom that was governed very wisely and fairly by an opposable finger. In other words, I guess you could say that this kingdom experienced a good rule of thumb.

79. People should be suspicious when they have a leader who radically tries to reinvent religious history. In other words, they should watch out for a loose canon.

80. Whenever a lion is king of the jungle, all of its animal followers have clean skin, and the wet season is plentiful. In other words, in regard to the lion, when it reigns, it pores.

81. Did you hear about the giant brick that was used to prevent ashes from floating into an air vent? It must have been a cinderblock.

82. I have a hard time divulging my emotions, when I'm on a train that doesn't make local stops. I guess it's just hard to express.

83. A lot of families stay at smaller hotels during vacations, because the bigger ones are more expensive. So, I guess you could say that people don't want to "resort" to paying more.

84. Did you hear about the military medical facility that only treated the highest-ranking officers? I guess you could say it was a general hospital.

85. There is a very rare organism that survives by breathing in people's mistakes. In other words, I guess you could say it breathes err.

86. One time, there was a queen who used her royal staff to catch anything that was thrown at her. This habit earned her the nickname "Inter-scepter."

87. Did you hear about the farmer who made a wheat-harvesting tool out of frozen soda? I guess you could say it was a pop-sickle.

88. One time, I found a small piece of burning coal that helped me to achieve deep dream sleep, and to recall my dreams the next morning. So, I guess you could say that I found a REM-ember.

89. I usually get annoyed watching melodramatic theater, because I'm very laid-back. So, I guess you could say I enjoy "mellow drama."

90. Did you hear about the man who found good employment working at a horse stall? I guess you could say he had a stable job.

91. Once, there was a group of birds who could learn extremely quickly while they were flying together as a unit. In other words, these birds were great at learning "in formation."

92. Did you hear about the man who tried to buy rollerblades for only $1? I guess you could say he was a cheapskate.

93. In some states, it's illegal for a newspaper to print an article unless the lettering has been adjusted to fit evenly within the margins. In other words, uneven formatting isn't "justified."

94. Once, there was an alien that ate canyons and was always hungry. In other words, I guess you could say it would "gorge" itself.

95. Did you hear about that guy who made a ton of money cooking steak tips? I guess you could say he made "ends meat."

96. One time, an 8-watt light bulb gave birth to a male deer, and then that deer traveled to a grade school where he met Sherlock Holmes. The deer asked Sherlock, "What kind of school is this?" To which Sherlock replied, "Elementary my deer watt son, elementary."

97. Mountain goats don't like using computers, because machines don't have enough RAM for them.

98. I've heard that some math teachers take off points on quizzes if students don't draw their graphs extremely neatly. I find that kind of grading pretty sketchy.

99. Did you hear about the arrow pouch that trembled whenever there was danger? I guess you could say the pouch was a quiver.

100. Did you know that Santa Claus met his wife during a stormy downpour? I guess you could say she was his rain dear.

101. In Judaism, there are some holidays where people aren't supposed to eat. Fortunately, the time goes by pretty fast.

102. One time, there was a rapper who had sparring matches with red vegetables. In other words, I guess you could say she was beet-boxing.

103. One time, my friend was caught speeding. The police officer issued him several tickets, as well as a literary bibliography. In other words, I guess you could say the officer gave my friend a number of citations.

104. One time, there was a man from Hawaii who became extremely out of control whenever he traveled to the mainland. So, I guess you could say he was very incontinent.

105. Did you hear about the journalist who lived in an underwater boat and had thousands of followers? I guess you could say people loved to "sub scribe" to her.

106. When you get a swollen lip, every word that you say sounds strange. In other words, your swelling is very pronounced.

107. A lot of people feel anxious in winter, but they relax again once spring returns and the trees all blossom. In other words, I guess you could say spring provides a great deal of re"leaf."

108. In a certain part of the world, male butterflies are extremely small and male moths are extremely large. However, the animals treat every male equally, be he butterfly or behemoth.

109. One time, all of the President's advisers decided to trim their nails during a meeting about inventory. So, I guess you could say the President met with a filing Cabinet.

110. Did you hear about the duck who had to put a wig on his beak, in order to fulfill his monthly rent? I guess you could say he needed "toupee" his "bill."

111. One time, I bought a glass container with a long neck, for mixing liquids. Then, one of my friends made a witty insult about my purchase. So, I guess you could say the conversation was full of "retorts."

112. Did you hear about the magic doctor's office, that conveniently appears whenever somebody needs to get a cavity filled? I guess the office is very coinci"dental."

113. Did you know that the same political family ran Chicago for over 40 years? People in other parts of the world might never have heard of this family, but if you live near Chicago, you hear about them on a Daley basis.

114. Once, there was a pig so sly that he convinced everyone he was human, and moved into a rich area in Scotland. In other words, this sly pig was more of a Cunningham.

115. Did you hear about the IRS agent who became exhausted at her desk? I guess you could say her job was very taxing.

116. One time, a group of people played a team sport in a pool, while they were wearing collared shirts. In other words, I guess you could say each person was involved in water polo.

117. Did you hear about the plastic surgeon who restructured his nostril, after he kept sticking his finger into it? He chose the new nostril shape from a design catalogue. In other words, he literally picked his nose.

118. I learned a lot about another country's culture, while I was coming back into the US through international airport security. So, I guess you could say I had a lesson in customs.

119. In cooking, a 'meringue' is a crisp sweet shell made of beaten egg whites. One time, I bent one of these shells into a V-shape, threw it into the air, and it returned back to me. So, I guess you could say I made a boomeringue.

120. Did you hear about the clock that patrolled the streets every night, stopping crime? I guess you could say this clock was really more of a neighborhood watch.

121. The Curse of the Bambino is a baseball superstition, about how the Boston Red Sox couldn't win a World Series for almost 90 years after they traded Babe Ruth. If the curse was real, then I'd certainly agree it was "Ruth"less to the Red Sox.

122. Did you hear about the man who sent a letter every day, as a matter of strict habit? I guess you could say he rote a lot.

123. Did you hear about the award that kept getting smaller over time? It started out as a statue, and then shriveled into a large cup, and then a plaque, and then "atrophy."

124. One time, to rebut an argument, I used a ruler to determine the length of my kitchen table. So, I guess you could say I took a "counter measure."

125. One time, a large car was being protected by a group of people who were developing new technology. In other words, this group of people was acting as a vanguard.

126. A girl owned a skirt that caused utter chaos. But, she only wore it in the month between April and June. So, I guess you could say that the chaotic skirt was really more of a mayhem.

127. Did you hear about the journalist who made all his own garments, by sewing together paper clippings from fashion magazines? He must have had many articles of clothing.

128. There was a small poster that was always displayed on airplanes. So, I guess you could say this poster was really more of a frequent flyer.

129. I have no idea where the word 'money' comes from. I wonder who first coined the expression.

130. One time, a man invented some soup that made people start giggling hysterically. In other words, the man invented a "laughingstock."

131. Did you know that the author of 'The Lord of the Rings' would often give small prizes to the people around him, as thank-you gifts? I guess these small gifts were really "tolkiens" of his appreciation.

132. Yesterday, I just wanted a clean and quiet room where I could think. So I visited eight different rooms, but no room in eight was clean and no "ruminate" was quiet.

133. Once, there was a man from Spain who bought many trains, because he was crazy. In other words, the Spaniard's purchase had some "loco motives."

134. There once was a priest who held rituals to heal people suffering from fluid-filled sacks. This priest was known as The Exor-cyst.

135. The last time I stayed at a hotel, I received a fruit basket free of charge. It even came with a note that said some nice things. In other words, I guess you could say the basket was "complimentary."

136. Did you hear about the two scientists who fell in love? They must have had good chemistry.

137. One time, a construction worker was hired to remove the top three floors from a building. In the middle of the job, he got a phone call that made him cry with joy. So, all in all, the construction worker shed a few tiers.

138. Did you hear about the queen who made excellent mathematical measurements?
She was truly a wonderful ruler.

139. I become very afraid whenever I transfer music from my laptop to my MP3 player. I guess you could say I get a syncing feeling in my stomach.

140. My computer can transform into an interstellar pub. All you have to do is hit the space bar.

141. An English teacher thought that grammatical mistakes were sinful, and so he made his students pay a fine whenever they made an error. His students called this fine a "syntax."

142. Did you hear about the dirty motel that was shaped like a fiddle? I guess you could say it was a vile inn.

143. I knew a man who had never done anything fairly in his entire life. So one time, he decided to be honest and impartial, merely to see what it felt like. In other words, I guess you could say he was "just out of curiosity."

144. Hollywood uses the same font for every movie poster. I guess you could say the font has been typecast.

145. My friend Megan goes temporarily insane after eating a certain spice in her food. Just a guess, but I imagine the spice is "nutmeg."

146. I used to know a guy who had all his garments made from pennies, nickels, and dimes. So I guess you could say that, no matter where he went, he always had a change of clothes.

147. An FBI agent who eats lots of donut is definitely a fed officer.

148. One time, my friend got a Bachelor of Science degree without doing any work. So, his degree was BS.

149. There have been too many politicians with mistresses in foreign countries. Ironically, the worst offender is on the committee of International Affairs.

150. A few weeks ago, I met three people who were eating German sausage. I didn't like any of the people, though, because one of them was a jerk, one was a fool, and one was a brat. I disliked the jerk a lot, I disliked the fool even more, and I disliked the bratwurst.

151. Did you hear about the lady who owned a pizza restaurant, and also had a side-job as a midwife? Her business slogan was "I deliver."

152. Once, there was a witch who tried to play tricks on people. Whenever someone fell for her tricks, she would turn that person into a seagull. In other words, people who were tricked were very gull-ible.

153. James Joyce was a famous writer. People stopped reading his books for a while, but recently he has become happily popular again. So, I guess you could say people are re-"Joyce"-ing.

154. I once knew a spine doctor who worked in the capital of Egypt. So, I guess you could say that this chiropractor was really more of a Cairo-practor.

155. One time at a restaurant, I ordered some Asian noodles. But then, the noodles started acting reckless and malicious. They must have been wanton.

156. Question: What does a pterodactyl have in common with a guy who urinates in the shower?
Answer: The pee is silent.

157. It look me years to lose 50 pounds, but I feel much better now, so the effort was definitely worth the weight.

158. Two pieces of land had identical width and length, but different height and temperature. In other words, they were fair in width and fair in length, but not "Fahrenheit."

159. I recently invented a new children's game, to help kids get to know each other. One kid chases a bunch of others around, trying to catch them. Any kid who gets caught becomes the new chaser. But the twist is, the kids need to introduce themselves every time they get caught. In other words, I've essentially invented "name tag."

160. Did you hear about the Turkish monarch who made a kingdom of padded footstools? I guess you could say that he ruled an ottoman empire.

161. Did you hear about the thorny red flower that learned to fly? It really rose to the occasion.

162. One time, I was talking to a frat guy at a college's Information Desk. I asked if there were any good restaurants in the area, and he said, 'Bro, no.' Then I asked if the sports teams were good, and he said, 'Bro, maybe.' Finally, I asked if I could see a pamphlet with a map of the campus; he gave one to me, and said, "Brochure."

163. There once was a woman couldn't sing by herself, but sang very well in a choir. The moral of the story? Good singing can be hard to an individual, but easy to "acquire."

164. I don't like empty countryside, because I find it too plain.

165. A magician could turn meat from a baby cow into meat from an adult cow. But, he would never reverse this process, because changing the meat back would expose the secret of the trick. So, the old saying is true: A magician will never re-"veal" his secrets.

166. I traveled to the top of a small mountain called Ment in Poland. Some friends and I were supposed to meet there, to see a band play. When I reached my destination, the band was there, but my friends had left. In other words, when I got to the top of the mountain, I found "abandonment."

167. Small sea organisms that drift are called 'plankton.' The adjective form of this term is 'planktonic.' One time, a pirate spilled an alcoholic drink onto a piece of wood, and that wood transformed into a bunch of small floating sea organisms. So, the spilled drink must have been "plank-tonic."

168. Did you know that France and the UK have almost exactly the same television stations? The only difference is, France has one extra station with TV shows that teach people how to speak the language of Britain. In other words, the only thing separating France from the UK is the English Channel.

169. A friend of mine--named Sal--is a big fan of Harry Potter, Russian history, and reptiles. So, one time, I gave Sal a snake dressed like a Pre-Soviet-era Russian monarch. In other words, I gave "Sal a czar slitherin'."

170. A famous debater once failed to make an argument about cutting down trees. I guess you could say she was stumped.

171. There once was a woman who never abbreviated her words with apostrophes, until she had a baby. The delivery must have given her contractions.

172. In a Navy training exercise, a captain used an underwater boat to force a surrender. In other words, I guess you could say the captain completed a "sub-mission."

173. It takes Santa a while to sort out the good deeds from the bad deeds, but eventually every deed gets sordid out.

174. Did you hear about the wilderness pioneer, who always wore a formal suitjacket as he hiked through forest paths? I guess his outfit was a real "trailblazer."

175. In a criminal case, an attorney needed to show that a mixed drink had a certain amount of alcohol by volume. I guess the lawyer suffered from a burden of "proof."

176. Jamaica has a large Jewish community, but the people there never eat bagels with smoked salmon because they dread lox.

177. Beneath the earth, dirt and rocks are organized into different layers called 'strata.' One time, an army general dug deep into the earth and extracted a bunch of rubies and diamonds, as part of an elaborate plan to confuse his enemies in battle. So, I guess you could say that the rubies and diamonds were part of the general's various "stratagems."

178. Did you hear about the dog that gave birth in the middle of a park? I guess she didn't read the sign not to litter.

179. I recently invented a giant Apple laptop that looks exactly like a hamburger. I'm going to call it the Big Mac.

180. Two scientists found a way to measure how old something is, while they were eating dinner together at a nice restaurant. So, I guess you could say they made progress in dating.

181. One time, a man broke his arm, and got a stiff surgical bandage around the bone. The surgical bandage was very wide, and it received television signals. So, I guess you could say the man received a "broadcast."

182. One time at a club, I saw a woman who had plants on all her clothing. When she danced, she had orchard fruits on her denim, and evergreen wood on her shoes. So, I guess you could say that she was wearing apple-bottom jeans and boots with the fir.

183. Certain kinds of bread make me sick. I guess you could say these bread types give ryes to stomach problems.

184. One time, in the season between winter and summer, I encountered a green and leafy herb. I wound this herb into a spiral shape, and then used it to bounce up and down. So, I guess you could say that I discovered "springthyme."

185. One time in a restaurant, a steak that I ordered was so rare, no one could find it.

186. Did you hear about the scam artist who parachuted out of a helicopter, and shouted obnoxious remarks to people as he fell toward the ground? All in all, the falling scam artist was very "con-descending."

187. I once knew a girl who jokingly used a very deep voice whenever she left phone messages. So, I guess you could say that she left voice male messages.

188. To 'dote' on somebody means 'to pamper excessively.' One time, I invented an elixir that stopped people from getting pampered. So, if excessive pampering is a bad thing, then I guess you could say I invented an "antidote" formula.

189. Did you hear about the doctor whose assistant was a big yellow dog? It must have been a "lab" technician.

190. One time, to show my affection for a girl, I painted poetry all around the city of Rome. The police said that they would arrest me if I tried those antics in Rome again, but what can I say? I'm a "Rome-antic" guy.

191. There is a certain apartment building that has incredible security on the fourth floor, between units 4B and 4D. In fact, the security is so tight that any breech would be un-4C-able.

192. There once was a man who became very indifferent, whenever he didn't keep an agenda of things to do. So, I guess you could say he was listless.

193. Did you know that liquor licenses have ID strips on them? This is to ensure that every pub keeps an accurate bar code.

194. Every time I donate money to wildlife charities, they send me a free t-shirt. I really wish they would spend my money on actually helping wildlife, instead of sending out merchandise. We're not going to save whales by giving a guy a hat, and we're not going to save sea cows by giving a "man-a-tee."

195. One time I went bowling with my friends, but instead of using a ball, I used the extra wheel from my car. The wheel knocked down all of the pins after two tries, but then I got so exhausted that I fell asleep. All in all, this incident was a great example of a "spare tire."

196. Fishermen invest a lot of money in the rope mesh that they use to catch animals at sea. I guess they appreciate net value.

197. In music, 'harmonics' are a type of vibration. Also, 'onyx' is a dark stone. People rarely carve onyx into musical instruments, because musical vibrations can damage the stone very badly. In other words, the dark stone is rarely used because the vibrations "harmonyx."

198. Navy Pier is a large tourist attraction in Chicago. I visited this attraction, with a friend who had dark blue skin. So, I brought a navy peer to Navy Pier.

199. England has just invented technology that turns precious stones into pure energy. Now, the Royal Family's riches can power all of London. In other words, London can be powered by the Crown Joules.

200. A bunch of tailors were all chatting online while they were sewing. I guess they had a long message thread.

201. For the last three nights, I've woken up to find a bunch of Chinese food in my lap, cooked in a bowl-shaped frying pan. I must be cooking the Chinese food while I dream. So, I guess you could say I'm sleep"wok"ing.

202. If a man doesn't get along with his in-laws, he usually can't stand coming over to their house more than a few times. He might act warm and extroverted the first three times that he comes to visit, but by the next visit, he won't act so "fourth coming."

203. A low-ranking nobleman ruled a desert patch of land. He must have had a baron designation.

204. There once was a magical chef who lived in an Emerald city, and measured all of his cooking ingredients in ounces. He was known as the Wizard of "Oz."

205. Did you hear about the man and woman who flirted with each other during a trial on a boat? Talk about a courtship…

206. My neighbor is so rich that she decided to cover her entire vegetable garden with gold paint. Now she has gold onions, gold peppers, and of course, a whole lot of gold "carats."

207. Automobile salesmen need to act charming and confident. In other words, you could say that they need to be "car-ismatic."

208. There once was a man who explored the insides of giant trees. He kept a diary of his exploits, writing down every time he went inside a trunk. So, the man kept a series of "log entries."

209. 'Wahl' is a small town in Luxembourg. One time, I built a tiny model of this town out of fine porcelain, and then used the model as a barricade. So, I effectively made a "grate Wahl of china."

210. I once knew a baseball player who made the most awful sound when he threw balls. Even worse, the balls themselves rarely landed where he wanted them to. So overall, he just suffered from a really bad "pitch."

211. Did you hear about the extremely sarcastic baker? All he made was wry bread.

212. Scientists in the capital city of The Republic of Ireland are trying to make a copy of the capital city of Northern Ireland. In other words, Irish scientists are "Dublin" Belfast.

213. Once, there was an island made of words, and its main business was producing clothing. So, the island had a "text isle" economy.

214. Scientists recently found a fossilized T-Rex that had been menstruating when it died. Researchers believe this skeleton dates back to the Jurassic "period."

215. There once was a boating team captain who was so physically powerful that whenever she gripped an oar, it would utterly explode in her fingers. So, you could say she was "robust."

216. Yesterday I saw a bird eat a large seed in just one gulp. The bird must have been a swallow.

217. Allergic reactions can cause skin irritation, if not something much worse. So at the very least, eating a food that you're allergic to can be a rash decision.

218. One time, the son of Odin forged a sharp weapon from the center part of an insect's body. This sharp weapon was known as a "thorax."

219. Since girls often complain that tall shoes are painful to wear, I've invented a stiletto that actually soothes the foot. I call it a high heal.

220. Question: What sound will a horse make if it eats a white, fluffy sandwich condiment?
Answer: "Mayo-neighs."

221. Did you hear about the villain whose sidekick was a tender steak? It must have been a filet minion.

222. Once a month, on the full moon, my home transforms into a giant storage facility. It must be a "were"-house.

223. I finally learned how hotdogs are really made. Since the process is usually so secretive, I welcomed the "frank" discussion.

224. If a fishing hook ever tried to play football, its position would probably be a tackle.

225. The green grouchy character from the TV show "Sesame Street" has been nominated for a major movie award. What a great Oscar nomination.

226. Gentlemen only wear clothes that can be dry-cleaned. If somebody even approaches gentlemen with laundry soap, they will run away. In other words, laundry soap acts as a "deter gent."

227. There's a new machine that improves the airflow in buildings, from within the ducts themselves. It wasn't easy to "in vent."

228. When two plants are competing for growth space, the plant with the stronger pollen usually wins. One time, a plant got exposed to radiation, and gained awesome superpowers. This plant's pollen spread far and wide. So, I guess you could say a super plant's pollen will "superseed" regular pollen.

229. I'm flattered whenever anyone gives me a gift of spicy sauce. I guess it's easy to curry favor with me.

230. Royal families often suffer from genetic diseases, because close relatives marry each other. So, I guess you could say the diseases are "heir-borne."

231. Two stalks of falling bamboo floated to the ground gently. This was possible because the two stalks were a "pair-o'-shoots."

232. I once knew a beautiful girl from the South who loved to eat enchiladas. In her community, she was known as the taco belle.

233. A dolly is a kind of small platform on wheels, used for carrying heavy objects. However, camels are better at carrying heavy things, and they also teach important lessons about spirituality. So, a camel is more like a "dolly llama."

234. One time, a woman hurt her hand while ripping the bark off a tropical coconut tree. So, I guess you could say two palms got hurt.

235. The Bering Strait is the small strip of water separating Russia from Alaska. I tried to find this water passage with a compass, but the needle kept getting stuck, so I never made it to my destination. In other words, I couldn't get my "bearing straight."

236. A soldier who yawns while in uniform is definitely fatigued.

237. One time, I made a delicious side-dish by shredding up lettuce, and then mixing it with ashes from my barbeque. So, I guess you could say I made coal slaw.

238. Police just found a male horned sheep chained to the wall of a rickety old apartment. So, I guess you could say the apartment was "ramshackle."

239. There once was an elementary school student who liked to stick things up his nose during his daily break from class. In other words, he made good use of his "recess."

240. One time, the nerves in my wrist got stiff and swollen because I was holding a steering wheel a lot, driving people back and forth on an enclosed road. So, my wrist injury came from carpool tunnel.

241. Did you hear about the plant that grows wax pastels as fruits? These fruits are called "crayon"-berries.

242. There once was a superhero who got incredibly strong on Saturday and Sunday. So, I guess Monday through Friday were his "weak"days.

243. One time, I competed in a tennis doubles tournament. Most people were assigned partners in advance, but I was not, so I didn't get a chance to practice properly before the competition. In other words, when I played in the tournament, I was not "pre-paired."

244. Did you hear about the man who seated himself on glossy fabric? I guess you could say he "satin" a chair.

245. I once found a small pixie trapped in the jewel of a pendant. I asked if the pixie wanted my help getting out, but the pixie said it didn't want any help because it liked being "in de pendant."

246. There once was a building that was supported by large columns of cocoons. In other words, I guess you could say the columns were cater-pillars.

247. One time, a pirate buried millions of gold coins at the base of a glacier. The pirate also left 15% of his loot on top of the glacier out of superstition, as a gratuity to thank the glacier for keeping the money hidden. Centuries later, sailors found the share of gold on top of the glacier, and they believed that this small gratuity was the entire treasure. Of course, in reality, this 15% of the gold was just the tip of the iceberg.

248. One time, I swallowed the reference section of a book. The pages made me ill, and a surgeon eventually needed to remove the reference section from my body. In other words, I had to get an appendix removed.

249. In certain swamps, people eat a white fluffy candy that makes them feel calm and relaxed. Due to this calming ability, the swamp candy has become known as a "marsh mellow."

250. I generally dislike dentists' offices. First the waiting room agonizes me with inactivity, then the doctor drills holes in my mouth. So, both halves of my appointment are very "boring."

251. One time, I had a bad dream about an armored fighter riding a female horse. In other words, I guess you could say that I encountered a "knight mare."

252. One time, at the Bathroom Olympics, the judges told a competitor, "On pooping, you're a ten. On washing, you're a nine. And on peeing, urinate."

253. The city of Istanbul has a good economy for ruby, emerald, and opal. Specifically, the market is steady in ruby, strong in emerald, and Constantinople.

Made in the USA
Lexington, KY
03 December 2016